ALL ABOUT THE MOON
(Phases of the Moon)
1st Grade Science Workbook

BABY PROFESSOR
EDUCATION KIDS

Speedy Publishing LLC
40 E. Main St. #1156
Newark, DE 19711
www.speedypublishing.com

Each month our Moon passes through eight phases.

A new moon is when the side of the moon facing the Earth is not illuminated. The Moon and the Sun are lined up on the same side of the Earth, so we can only see the shadowed side.

Because the moon takes almost the same amount of time to complete one revolution as it does one rotation, we see mainly the same side of the moon at all times.

A waxing crescent moon
is when the Moon looks
like crescent and the
crescent increases in size
from one day to the next.

When the Moon, Sun,
and Earth line up,
an eclipse occurs.

The first quarter moon
means that the Sun
and the Moon make
a 90-degree angle
compared to the Earth.

Gravity on the moon
is only about 1/6
of that on Earth.
If you drop a rock
on the moon, it
falls more slowly.

A waxing gibbous moon occurs when more than half of the lit portion of the Moon can be seen. The Moon remains in the sky most of the night.

The moon
has its own
time zone.

A full moon is when the Moon is brightest in the sky. This is also the time of the lunar month when you can see lunar eclipses.

A second full moon
in one calendar
month is usually
called a "blue moon"
and this occurs
approximately
every 3 years.

A waning gibbous moon is
less than fully illuminated,
but more than half.

The Earth, seen
from the moon,
also goes through
phases.

The last quarter moon
is when the Moon has
reached half illumination.

On average the
Moon moves at
2,288 miles per hour
around Earth.

A waning crescent moon
is the final sliver of
illuminated moon we can
see before the Moon
goes into darkness again.

The moon's orbit
around Earth is an
oval, not a circle,
so the distance
between the center
of Earth and the
moon's center
varies throughout
each orbit.

The moon is not round. Instead, it's shaped like an egg.

Tides on Earth are
caused mostly
by the moon.

Visit
BABY PROFESSOR
EDUCATION KIDS
www.BabyProfessorBooks.com
to download Free Baby Professor eBooks
and view our catalog of new and exciting
Children's Books